Art Director, Nature Humphries
Author photo: Kathryn Mayo

For information or bulk sales, contact Nautilus Publishing, 426 South Lamar Blvd., #16, Oxford, MS 38655

ISBN: 978-1-949455-29-8

First Edition

Printed in the United States of America

For my Grandchildren

Sophie Patricia Strand

Lois Elizabeth Reeves

Jonah Clement Strand

Anne Smith Reeves

TABLE OF CONTENTS

FOREWORD

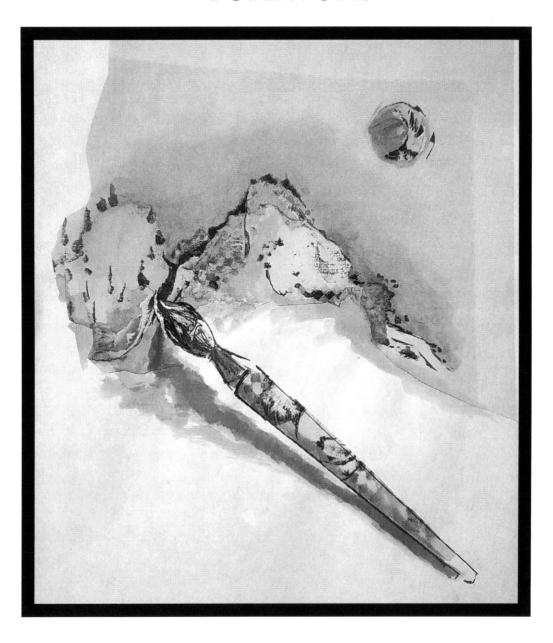

Once upon a time there was a little girl with a little crayon right in the palm of her hand. And when she was good she was very, very good. And when she was bad she drew all over the walls. And when she was five, she painted the porch steps pink with the oil-based paint that she mixed from the cans of red and white that the house painter had left open in the backyard. But luckily, instead of being squelched for her actions, her parents loved her creativity and encouraged it, just as she will love and encourage yours as she invites you to enhance or reconnect to your own innate, creative spirit within these pages and beyond.

This book is for all who want to feel aware and alive within, whether they are religious or not. It is for all those on the human journey who want to feel connected to themselves, to others, and to the universe. Although I have used language that will be familiar to some but not others, it describes states of being found across many faiths and most cultures. The routes we take on our own particular journeys are personal, but the experiences are universal. It is to welcoming these universal experiences that this work is directed.

One: BEGINNING

. . . swinging high, flying way up, higher than real life
. . . I look down, I see all the ordinary stuff . . . the
porch, the toolshed . . . the clothesline, the
chinaberry tree. But they are lit up from inside so
that their everyday selves have holy sparks in them,
and if people could only see those sparks, they'd go
and kneel in front of them and pray and just feel
good. Somehow the whole world felt like little
altars everywhere.

—Rebecca Wells

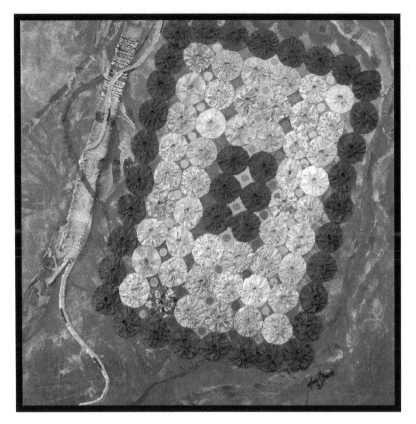

PLATE 1: THE SWING

When I found this early twentieth-century doll bed quilt made entirely of feed sack yo-yos, I immediately felt delight and thought of experiences of childhood and play. And then its shape gave me the idea of a child's chair swing, and playful streamers came into mind. Strangely, the tiny dots of light nestled between the yo-yos were placed there before I paired the painting with one of my favorite quotations, but as I looked more closely, they seemed to echo little altars everywhere and the holy sparks of childhood.

A problem arises when we become socialized: we often lose our connection to the sacred wonder of the world. Not only do we lose our connection to the holy energy outside of ourselves, but also we become unplugged from that same energy inside—our own authentic voice and the essence of who we were in the first place!

Disconnected from our confidence, we forget that "being me and you" is okay. We tend to lose that original, authentic identity under a deluge of messages about what is right or wrong! So much so that what was once a calling from deep down inside may now be only a faint whisper.

In this book, I talk about trusting and being your authentic Self, a message that is woven into the fabric of this book.

One of the greatest gifts I have received in the last few years is a story that artist Donna Pickens told me about my Atlanta art class. In 1979, after I left the city to move north with my family, Donna and four other members of the group (some even novices, having discovered their individual styles) used their talents to start their own art gallery. And, equally as important, with each acting as their authentic artist self they had kept it going successfully for seven years—a great accomplishment in the art world.

As I look back I realize that what delighted me then, and seems always to have been my calling, was guiding myself and others in finding and nurturing that fragile connection—so easily lost—of staying with or becoming reconnected to our own unique Selves, to others, and to the sacred energy of the universe.

> *Connection is why we are here. It gives purpose and meaning to our lives.*
>
> —*Brene Brown*

Neurobiologically, we are wired to connect, both internally and externally, to our place in this universe. When we fear we are unworthy of connection, we do not have a place. We are lost.

I have always had a fear of being lost. When I was four years old, my mother dropped me off at a strange place where I was badly hurt. Of course, she did not know the place was dangerous or she would never have left me there. Still I wound up being a different child when I came home that day—feeling existentially lost, disconnected, with all my fuses blown.

When my life-giving father suffered a massive heart attack at forty-one and died of another, one month after he turned forty-four and shortly after my fourteenth birthday, I became depressed and further disconnected from the flame of childlike joy within, although you couldn't tell because I looked okay on the outside.

The next year I even won Miss St. Francis County—chosen by the lodgers at Carl's Courts, the local motel there (in fact, the only motel there) owned by, yes, Carl, so there would be no prejudice by the locals as to who was chosen! That is Arkansas for you, just trying to be fair and square. But as you might imagine, I was not doing me. I was performing. On the inside, I knew something was radically wrong.

The making and sharing of art has been a redemptive process for me—my journey into awareness and what some Native Americans call a soul retrieval.

In this soul retrieval, I rediscovered a joyful oneness.

Author Richard Rohr likes to tell this old joke: *A mystic walks up to a hot dog vender and says, make me one with everything.*

After he gets a laugh, I imagine, Richard tells us this joke really misses the point because ... We are already one with everything. All that is absent is awareness.

The mystic's command to the hot dog vender,

Make me one with everything,

reaffirms the realization for me that—

    if we are all one,

        nobody can be lost—

            we are all at home already.

Forty years ago we moved to New Jersey, where my husband was headmaster of a school founded in 1774—its mascot a portrait of a literal "minute man" with a musket, a tri-cornered hat, and strapped books carried under one arm. Close to New York City, we explored Chinatown one crisp fall afternoon. There I found some beautiful paper at a Chinese grocery store. It had brilliant metallic gold and bright saffron ink rectangles stamped with red lines on thin pale natural paper. With no idea what the paper was made for or how I could get more, I had been using it for a series called The Imaginary Landscape, which explores the mystery behind reality and its connection to the divine realm.

One day much later, I saw a UNICEF Christmas card made from that same paper. On the back it said, "made from Chinese spirit paper." I looked up the name and discovered its traditional use: a ceremonial paper for making contact with the ancestors. It was meant for reconnecting to what had been lost! When burned, its smoke was thought to carry messages to a divine realm.

Not knowing its nature, all those years I had been using the beautiful paper for the similar purpose of making contact with what had been lost in my own life and the lives of others. Today, when writing this, I thought of my father.

◆

PLATE 2: MIXED-MEDIA COLLAGE WITH CHINESE SPIRIT PAPER

When I was thirty-nine, while we were still in Atlanta, with the support of my husband, mother, and nurse maid Eula Mae, I took an educational sabbatical. I left Allan and the four children for the summer to go to the New York Studio School in Paris to study with painter Elaine de Kooning, art teacher, critic, and famous artist in the Expressionist movement.

Needless to say, this was a fabulous experience. In the Studio School, you sculpted the figure, you painted the figure, and you drew the figure. They did not give you a scarf or a hat or anything to add to the nude figure to enhance the composition, and they did not give you anything behind the figure but a blank, charcoal-smudged wall.

One day after painting a model standing on a worn green desk, I told my teacher, Elaine, who had by then become a mentor, that it looked to me like a nude standing on a green desk at the Holiday Inn. She told me something that I will never forget: "Anne, you're missing the point—even a nude standing on a green desk at the Holiday Inn has a spiritual quality when you've painted it. You need to look at that fact and not forget it!"

I believed her, and when I did, a piece of myself came home.

This book, with its images, meditations, and quotations, I offer as an invitation to journey into stillness, to the wonder of the light, and to the retrieval of the lost pieces of our Selves. In this book, journeying is another term for awakening—a journey to which I whole-heartedly invite you.

Reclaiming what has been lost and finding the courage to return to ourselves brings us into authenticity, wonder, and oneness. It gives us what philosopher Paul Ricoeur called a second naiveté, an innocence born of a depth of experience rather than ignorance.

I think you may have heard something like this before…

"*Verily, I say unto you,*
        unless you become transformed
           and become as little children
    you will not
        enter the kingdom of heaven."

⊙ Two: BECOMING

Saint Frances said to the apple tree,
    "Speak to me of God,"
And the apple tree blossomed.
       —*anonymous*

In a period of quiet alertness, the infant experiences a state of relaxed wakefulness. Here the parent has succeeded in providing the nurturing support needed for perfect containment. I love the idea of relaxed wakefulness, not just for infants but for all of us.

Relaxed wakefulness is a metaphor for traditional enlightenment—a form of having no anxiety about tomorrow, being here now, being at home in our bodies to the oneness of all that there is. Further, to be in a state of relaxed awakefulness—all right, I added the a—we must become both the child and the parent of our own Selves. But, how do we do this? Just how do we call forth this state of relaxed awakefulness?

For me—because I couldn't get out of my own way and stop the unceasing word bath from flooding my waking consciousness—I needed to parent myself by resorting to traditional meditation as a form of soul retrieval. The "word bath" I refer to is sometimes called monkey mind in meditation circles.

It looks like this: We are in a house with twenty other people walking briskly from room to room, each speaking in a voice that can be easily heard by the other occupants upon passing. First you hear from inside your own head, *Did I give lunch money to…Did I leave a note for…* And from another quarter, *What the hell did he mean by that?* And then, *That report is due at five o'clock, I'll never finish it!* Or, *She does it over and over to me, again this morning, last week, when will she realize that…* And from over your shoulder, *Why did I do that?* Or a little louder, *If I stop at noon, I can just pick it up in time before…*

Few people live in the present moment. Unaware of their immediate surroundings, they sleepwalk through life with just enough waking radar to keep from knocking into the furniture.

Monkey mind means living in the jumble of the past or the future and missing the present. You may even recognize it in yourself. If so, you know there can be many voices in our one head. It becomes even worse when we begin to identify with and believe the thoughts that tromp through our brains, many of which routinely convey the same messages, recycling and meaningless. These thoughts get in our way, preventing us from experiencing the relaxed awakefulness we need to find the peace that has been lost, hiding behind the patter.

In traditional meditation, we agree to sit quietly with eyes closed or slightly open. Perhaps crossed legged or in a chair, for a minimum of twenty minutes, emptying our minds. This of course puts people off and makes them feel like a failure, because you can't empty your mind unless you are a highly trained practitioner. You can just let it flow until something comes up again. Letting go is a better example for what happens here. Not holding on, not retaining. Occasionally, the gaps in between breaths are moments of quiet. Perhaps they grow longer the more you develop your practice. But thoughts intrude and you must bring yourself home again and again on the path, as kindly as though you were a little child.

Of course, when I started, I used meat hooks to bring my child back to the path. Harsh and unkind and not at all what a child needs. Eventually I turned into a different parent and I lead myself compassionately as time progressed, gently and kindly back toward the path.

When I began to practice traditional breath-counting meditation—counting on the intake of the breath from one to four, repeated for a period of twenty minutes twice a day—I didn't realize then that it was possible to climb into the present moment periodically many times a day. I thought I had to do at least twenty minutes at a time. But now I know we can experience relaxed awakefulness by stepping into small moments of silence—finding and retrieving the lost parts of our Selves through stillness and sliding into the senses—the current notion of mindfulness.

No one is devaluing a traditional meditation practice. But it is important to note that just a few high-quality moments of awareness of sensory stillness can grow into more each day, making life sweeter. To focus on awareness, even in small quantities, enlivens the quality of our life experiences. A gentle if quick return to the present moment can nourish and satisfy us on multiple levels, and as a result, we can in turn nourish others and the earth.

So—meditation or mindfulness? One practice is not better than the other. They are different. But this journey will focus on mindfulness.

A meditation practice can be a wonderful thing. For many who choose it as a path, it can become a blessed gift. And so it was for me. After a year or so, I began to experience what I can only call "the peace that passeth all understanding," an actual shift in energy within, moving down out of my head and dropping through my body, into my legs and feet, grounding me to the earth in a feeling of safety and oneness. In fact, unless I were to move a part of my body, I could not tell where I stopped and the outside world began. In those mystical moments I had escaped the trap of my thinking momentarily to get out of my own way. I could then begin to experience what had been there all the time—what some call the "kingdom of heaven within."

The great psychoanalyst Carl Jung said that just one such experience is enough to build a whole life around. Some experiences can create a 180-degree turn, a metanoia, or going in a different direction. And such it was for me.

At this point I realized that "becoming as a little child" was not a job for the intellect and that I, like Job discovered for himself, did not have a high-level eagle's eye view with which to judge all of creation. It had begun to dawn on me that Winnie the Pooh and I were more alike than I had thought, and that in the scheme of things—black holes and all—that I was "a bear of very little brain."

A brilliant scientist once cautioned me, "Anne, what you just don't realize is that we as humans are nothing but motes."

"I do realize that," says I, "and what you don't realize is that it takes the pressure off!"

Now, I would change that to mote-sized diamonds, however—all of us together, sparkling in the great net of being, connected to one another, past, present and future, to the eternal, and to the depth and height of the great divine presence that permeates and sustains us all.

Does everyone have to perform serious spiritual discipline to experience Jung's moment of transcendence? The answer is both yes and no.

No to traditional meditation, whirling dervishing, or sitting on a mountain top for years at a time, but yes to becoming aware, brushing the cobwebs out of consciousness and getting out of our own way in order for us to recognize and experience—like the power of the ruby slippers worn by Dorothy in the Land of Oz—what has been in the background, waiting for us all along.

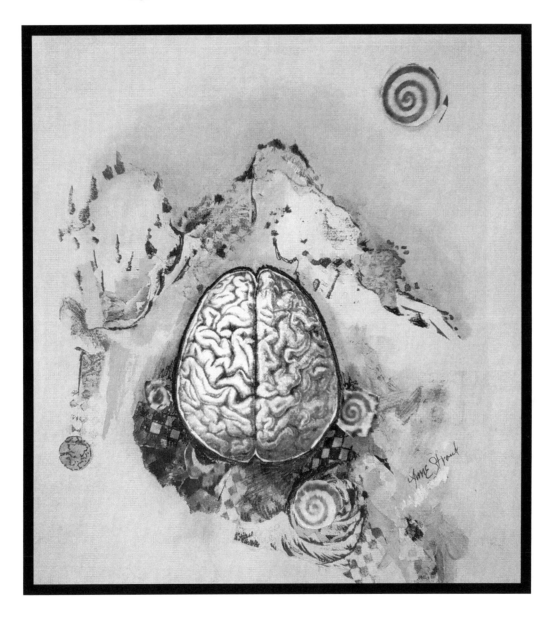

Wholeness is not achieved
by cutting off a portion of one's being,
but by [the] integration of contraries.
—*Carl Jung*

The morning of December 10, 1996, Jill Bolt Taylor, PhD, brain research scientist at the Harvard Brain Bank and author of *My Stroke of Insight*, felt an intense pain stab her brain directly behind her left eye. Immediately she felt a sense of dissociation come over her, but not realizing the seriousness of her situation, she decided to shake it off, take a shower, and get ready for work! As her symptoms worsened and her right arm became impaired, she thought, "I'm having a stroke." And then she reported thinking inside herself, "Wow, how many scientists have the opportunity to study their own brain function and mental deterioration from the inside out?"

At this point, Dr. Taylor's entire professional life had been dedicated to understanding the workings of the human brain, and now she was actually having (what she later entitled her book) a remarkable stroke of insight! When she finally arrived at the hospital after much delay, she was diagnosed with a massive stroke that had destroyed much of her left brain functioning.

Our brains have two separate hemispheres that can operate

independently. They are connected by a small band between the two. Although they are equal in size and shape, they do not perform the same functions, and they serve the body in different ways.

The left brain hemisphere controls the right side of the body. So, when Dr. Taylor's right arm failed her, it was not surprising that she was diagnosed with a stroke of the left hemisphere.

The left brain allows us to see the world in parts. It analyzes, computes, labels, and thinks. It performs tasks pertaining to mathematics and language and is the more academic and logical side of the brain.

The right brain hemisphere controls the left side of the body. It sees in wholes and perceives connections between things. It intuits and performs tasks that have to do with creativity, wonder, oneness, and the arts.

Once I had an eighty-year-old mentor, physician Lila Bonner-Miller, who went back to school at age sixty to change specialties and become a psychiatrist. Lila was a person who knew how to be her "Self." She was dedicated, original, and she radiated wonder and energy as she moved through the world. At times, when she did not recall something, she would say, "I'll just turn it over to my right brain and I'll have the answer in twenty minutes." Under her tutelage, I began to trust the right brain.

The right brain is the seat of experiencing oneness and belonging. It sees in wholes and not in parts. It is our connection to the heart. It can't label, can't even name, but it knows what things are for and can appreciate the bittersweet loveliness of the world. Through it we can slide into the wonder of our senses and experience the joy of being. In fact, this is the stroke of insight that Jill Taylor discovered! She had discovered it involuntarily by experiencing the source of oneness.

> *"The neurological circuitry located in our right brain is constantly running and always available for us to hook into as the seat of peace and oneness."* —Jill Bolt Taylor

Scientific research has shown that when the language center of the left brain is quieted, we can get out of monkey mind. Further, when we experience the right brain circuitry—which is always up and online—we can feel relaxed awakefulness.

Now, no one is saying for us to stop using our left brains. That would be disastrous. Nor are we saying the right brain is better than the left brain! But in Western society, left brain use is so heavily weighted that we have neglected our right brain and have become human *doings* rather than human *beings*. An ongoing dialogue between the two hemispheres is required. We need an interactive circuitry—like the infinity symbol—communicating over and over through this neurological band for a perfect balance between the two halves of the whole of our brains.

The left brain is the seat of the ego. This ego, or what Carl Jung calls the small-letter self, tries to keep us safe in the world of history—the chronological time of clocks ticking and calendars marching. It gets us there on time, balances our checkbooks, and worries for us.

The problem comes because the ego thinks it is the only one in charge and is fearful because it thinks it is alone and separate. Becoming ego-driven causes us to unplug from enchantment in our daily lives, to have our inner light go out, or to feel cut off with no other reliable source. Without our ego's management, however, enchantment alone can cause us to overdraw our budget, or even worse, to become poor negotiators of the ordinary world.

When we intentionally turn things over to our right brain with a momentary stillness pause, we will find it is the seat of our openness to God, intuition, spirituality, and oneness. This repeatable event presents the perfect tool for creating an opening into the possibility that God is not the stressful, judging power we may remember from our particular cultural background. With this momentary break, we can escape from our history and the tyranny of our left brain's ego by spanning the ribbon that connects us to our right brain and the experience of oneness.

By relaxing into awareness, we can a realize that God or spirit permeates our day-to-day existence and exists in everything. So, instead of being stuck thinking of a world founded on a harsh judging energy, we can detour into the love energy at the source of everything.

Here we can experience the comfort of the right brain, let go of all the labeling judgement, settle down, and become childlike enough to feel its nurture.

This presence comes to us through the relaxation of the left brain's thought machine. This discovery of the right brain's ongoing soul music connects us to a power greater than ourselves. It can open us to the fact that all creation is pierced by a presence that transcends our egos and plugs us directly into the vibrant energy of a world of mystery and of joy.

◆

LOVE
> *is the core energy*
>> *that rules everything.*

LOVE
> *is the one ingredient*
>> *that holds us all together.*
>>> *—John E Fetzer*

37

PLATE 3: STARRY NIGHT

Scientists tell us that we are made of the same substances as the stars. I like that. Song-writers tell us that "love makes the world go 'round." I like that, too. The stitches on this single quilt square tell me that we are held together in a beautiful design with perfect skill and patience, each different, and unique, and loved, and wanted, and made of stars, shining all together in the starry night.

38

A neurological circuitry of love energy resides in our right brain. Perhaps we should reject our judgmental images of God and change to a circuitry of love energy described as constantly running, like a warm comforter. It is always there but is often masked by the litany of our left-brain override.

> *Now, it might be that your God is an uptight,*
> *judgmental perfectionist…*
> *If this is your God,*
> *maybe you need to blend in someone who is ever so slightly more*
> *amused by you, someone less anal…*
> *for instance, Gracie Allen is good. Mr. Rogers will work.*
> —*Anne Lamott*

The left brain's ego cuts off, separates, judges, and labels things as right or wrong, as either/or, and as good or bad when it ain't necessarily so.

A famous country singer philosopher illustrates this point with humor when she quips:

The way I see it, if you want the rainbow, you gotta put up with the rain.

—Dolly Parton

The ability to note the raindrops without judgement is a gift of the Stillness Break and entering the right brain. Freed from the ego's need to split the world into good and bad—and tasting all day of the duality of the tree of the knowledge of good and evil—we can delay judgement and become aware in the moment.

When we see the world as all or nothing and either/or, our rainbow has only two poles, two options, black or white, wrong or right. When we experience the world as both/and, we have many available options. We can have all the colors of the rainbow!

The ego with its labeling encyclopedia of our left brain can interfere with peacefulness, but is a wonderful tool when we need it. Our right brains have the power to consult and use the tools and skills of the left brain at any time. The problem comes when we forget that the left brain is a servant-asset and not in charge of everything.

The ego is sometimes referred to as the false self, but it is only false because it has the wrong title and the wrong job description. Ego thinks of itself as the president with responsibility for everything, while, in reality, it is a magnificent set of tools. We need the gift of the ego to help us function in the world of time and space. This gift helps us evaluate, organize, succeed, and much, much more.

However, danger lurks in this confusion about our title and our job description—no matter how gifted we are. If we allow our ego to keep thinking it is the president, trying to stay in charge of everything rather than facilitating a greater plan, the ego will buckle under the stress and pressure, become anxious, despondent, and maybe worse—the classic, old-fashioned nervous breakdown. Consequently, it will fail to move us along in our worldly tasks.

As a result of this confusion, our ego will block our ability to live authentically. It will keep us from using our intuition, our innate knowledge, and our whole Self in negotiating life. And it will separate us from our God-given higher power energy and guidance.

41

When we put the proverbial cart (toolbox) before the horse (power) it can turn into a virtual disaster.

When some traditions call for us to "die to ourselves before we physically die," they are calling for us to demote our ego, to stop it from thinking that it is the president. It calls for us to become as a little child again and to trust the wisdom of our whole Self, connected and in balance.

By becoming connected to the eternal empowering energy of the universe, our higher power—or God as we understand God—we open the space for divine love energy to flow through us, with nothing cut off. We discover that the promise of resurrection is true for each of us, now. The ego's presidency can die, be reborn, and be taken over by the higher power always waiting in the wings.

By rediscovering the oft-forgotten gift of our right brain, we can begin to trust that connection to a power beyond ourselves, a gift that keeps on giving and can never be destroyed—we can be transformed to live in integration, balance, belonging, and love.

"Verily I say to you that unless you become transformed and become as little children you will not enter the Kingdom of Heaven."

For when we are made one with everything, sacred altars spring up everywhere, and we are not alone anymore. Nobody can be lost. We are at home already!

◆

Once when I was caught cycling in my ego, I thought I was in charge of ultimate rightness and wrongness! As I was struggling with the words of a certain creed, a dear spiritual mentor, Episcopal priest and seminary professor Nelson Thayer, told me the finger that points to the moon is not the moon, and sometimes words merely symbolize that which lies beyond in the mystery.

At that moment, because I trusted his judgement and his wisdom, I realized I did not have to struggle with the words that troubled me but could surrender to the mystery—to where the words were pointing—the majesty of which is unintelligible to the logic of the human mind.

I also realized that perhaps we live in a world filled with many fingers pointing to the moon—of all colors and from all faiths—many thinking they are the moon, some thinking they have creeds with the only right words and answers, some even starting wars over it, and then there are some who know that we are all in this together, sustained by a divine providence that loves us all.

Balancing our left and right brain hemispheres can take us to the place where we can experience the world in this way—a world filled with wisdom and agency, the portal to Spirit and the peace that passes all understanding. Taming the left brain's ego (its need for titles and making a name for itself) and befriending the right brain's oneness is the stuff of re-enchantment, balance, and the co-creation of a sacred world.

Life is not a matter of creating
a special name for ourselves,
but of uncovering the name
we have always had.

—Richard Rohr

The golden moments in the stream of life
rush past us, and we see nothing but sand;
the Angels come to visit us,
and we only know them when they are gone.
　　　　　　　　　　—George Eliot

PLATE 4: THE GOLDEN MOMENT: PAST, PRESENT AND FUTURE

It seemed to me as I was

envisioning this work,

that each of us has a sacred challenge—to become who we are des-
  tined to be within the only time we are given that power

—the precious, fleeting,

Golden Moment of the Now—

for the past is over

and the future is dependent

on the "NOWS"

of what will soon be past.

But—how can we do this—

  have the chance of actually capturing

    the NOW?

Most of us love steps.

One, two, three…

Conceptual sequences.

We can commit these to memory, do them diligently for a few days, put them on a list to do this week or to achieve some time in the future, or just forget about them.

The steps we are exploring, however, are not about doing, they are about being.

Not about learning but about unlearning. Not about building but about finding.

These are pathways on the journey into awareness. "Baby steps," if you will. They are built on trust and require falling, laughter, and self-forgiveness. They are not something to achieve but a way of finding what is there already. Each requires a lifting of judgment and an appreciation of what is now. These simple actions pave the way for us to awaken and to become reacquainted with wonder.

Sometimes the voice of the ego in our head is so pervasive that it is easily mistaken for the whole of us. That is, until we have become "still" enough to experience something beyond its judging chatter. The voice that matters is that of awareness and consciousness. Awareness comes by practicing stillness long enough to learn the difference between the ego's voice and our true connected Self.

A friend told me about a time he tried to go on a silent retreat. Unfortunately, it is a familiar story. You may recognize it in yourself. He had planned to enjoy the time off just to be with himself but the judging, driving voice in his head would give him no peace. He felt worse than ever when he finally gave up and escaped.

He was a very successful man who had spent his whole life always doing—always running, always busy, and always afraid not to fill every waking moment with planning for the future and collecting new things, from automobiles to women, just so he could escape that inner voice and its critical thinking.

That is what many of us are afraid of—
BEING WITH OUR SELVES.

And just how do we learn to be with our Selves?

We do it in small moments of silence, through entering our senses, so we do not become overwhelmed. We learn to care for our Selves with tender wisdom. Going to the gym, overdoing it, and getting so sore we can hardly walk or get injured, ensures that we will not be returning to that space for a while. And so it is with stillness. We ease into awareness through our senses until stillness welcomes us, not in a way that clubs us over the head.

Start easing into awareness by just noticing in your daily life what surrounds you! For example, while in the bath or shower, feel the water on your skin, simply be with the experience of the water as it cools or warms you, watch as it flows from the tap or trickles through your fingers. Feel the air touch your body as you step out. Breathe in and enjoy the steam or the rich scent of the soap. Experience the texture of the towel as you dry and wrap your body and register what it feels like to be really clean! Basically, just be at home in yourself and your surroundings.

You may find yourself feeling grateful for the privilege of bathing, for hot water, for time, for privacy. Now, pause and listen to what you hear and see around you.

> *It is our heightened state of awareness*
> *that lets us connect to whatever we are doing*
> *and reconnects us to the richness of being.*

So, mindfulness, the word so many people use today, is replaced with the Stillness Break. Our minds are not full but in a period of being let go, moving, in flow. They are open and waiting for what is to come.

Pausing for a Stillness Break creates an opportunity to mine the treasure of the right brain—the deeper Self constantly operating and waiting for our visit. It acts as the comforter, the sacred connecter to a power greater than ourselves.

✦

The Stillness Break

Slip into the senses by becoming aware of your surroundings, whatever is near you right now.

SEE: Look around. Pay close attention to what you see. The color of the sky, the movement of leaves outside your window, the blue of the wall, the violet of the scarf on the chair, the pattern on a piece of paper crumpled on the floor. Try seeing with no judgment, just awareness.

HEAR: The hum of the refrigerator, a bird outside chirping, the rustling of the wind in the trees, the beeping of a truck backing up, the whir of an insect's wings, a train whistle far away. No stories, just awareness.

SMELL: Breathe in. Literally, wake up and smell the coffee, a faint hint of honeysuckle, (if you are lucky) the sweet smell of a freshly bathed baby's skin, the hickory smell of a fire pit outside, something that needs emptying in the trash. No judgment in the NOW, just awareness.

FEEL: The heat of the sun on your skin, the chilled glass against your palm, the texture of a book's pages, the feeling of your shoes on your feet, your head on a pillow, or the petals of a rose.

TASTE: A mint leaf from the garden, the salt from a peanut, fresh water from the tap, your first cup of tea for the day, a grape, a raisin.

Feel appreciation for these experiences with wonder, as new, like a child.

Become aware of as few or as many of these tiny quality events of consciousness as you wish—no pressure. Quantity is not the issue here. Delight in your senses; noticing is the pathway that releases you from worry. Feel momentary joy for what you just became aware of—the sky, the bird's song, water. If there is no joy felt right now, there is no judgement. We are grateful just that we stopped to feel. That is enough.

This is the essence of the Stillness Break.

It forms the yellow brick road that strengthens our connection, building it, brick by brick, to the power that leads us to experiences of enlightenment.

In fact, ending these moments with gratitude is now the basis for most, if not all, the abundance thinking so currently popular. Abundance nests in the arms of gratitude—an ancient lyric sung by contemporary voices.

Another way to slip into the senses and experience awareness is to feel the living energy inside our bodies—a wonderful way to bind anxiety.

One way to begin to experience this energy is to put our arms and hands out in front of us and close our eyes. Since we can't see them, how do we know our hands are there?

When we are still and aware and wait for a moment, we can most likely feel the energy and the aliveness inside of them. And we can learn to bring this awareness of being into our whole body.

Feeling the breath as it enters our nose and makes our lungs expand is always a delightful part of being in the inner body. The breath joins the universe inside of us to the universe outside as atoms bombard each other in the lively, aerated dance of life.

This practice of experiencing the felt sense of being has been very helpful to me personally. Strangely, I have found it impossible to feel anxious when putting my attention inside and focusing on my inner body experience of aliveness, of molecule bumping into molecule in a spiritual do-si-do.

We are slowed down sound and light waves,
a walking bundle of frequencies
tuned into the cosmos.
We are souls dressed up
in sacred biochemical garments
and our bodies are the instruments
through which our souls play their music.
—Anonymous

Although stopping for a few moments each day adds up to very few actual minutes, these tiny doses of loving kindness can bring us gentle escape from suffering.

We do this by accepting where we actually are, not where we wish to be or feel we should be. The non-acceptance of immediate reality causes us to suffer.

Suffering differs from pain. Suffering is not based on the reality of the situation itself but on the story we tell ourselves about it. To escape the stories of monkey mind for a moment and take a break from suffering, we can take these ancient pathways toward peace.

We can choose the realization that we are actually safe here in this brief moment, and we do not need to worry, problem solve, or interpret—although these thoughts will naturally float through our heads. When they do, we can expect it without being alarmed. We can kindly remember that our thinking left brain is always trying to protect us and goes on and on and on.

When we suffer from over-thinking, it is helpful to close our eyes and sit quietly with our back straight and our feet flat on the floor. (This can also be done in bed.)

Relaxing our body as much as possible, simply wait for the next thought to come up. As a thought comes into our mind, let it rise and watch it float away up into the imaginary sky of the mind, like a cloud, or a bubble, or a leaf, and drift away right out of the picture into a stream of air.

Flowing water works to help wash excess thinking right out of the way. We are not trying to stop the thoughts, only to let them go, only not to hold on to them, nor get trapped by them. To resist them makes them persist. To let them move through cleanses the channel. Then we merely watch and wait for another one to come along and see what happens.

When we settle in and are curious of what will come next, letting each one of them peacefully float through, they will tend to slow down and lessen of their own accord. If it is important it will come back later at a better time. No judgement is needed, only attention.

(Although this method is used in traditional meditation, it can be used as a Stillness Break for us during our days and nights.)

As we practice these pathways several times a day, our awareness grows. Being more present in the here and now, rather than lost in the past or daydreaming about the future, we may begin to more deeply understand the stories we tell ourselves about our past or project into our futures.

When we go into a state of relaxed awakefulness, at home in the present moment, we often begin to notice that the journey of our own personal history fades into a state of belonging. As our story becomes more flexible and open, we become more connected and loving, and we enter the greater story with our lives. This is not something to do but something to be surprised and relieved by—a gift.

When we are no longer alone in our individual story, but have become a part of the greater story, we are held, safe, and one with the all. (This experience is fleeting, and it is supposed to be.) But we can return to it over and over as we practice these simple breaks. Most religions promise us this experience, and it is available to and found by many people throughout the world. It is the ground of being and the pearl of great price. It is as near to us as our own body.

The only journey is within.
                                        —*Rilke*

If there is to be peace in the universe…

there must be peace in the world…

If there is to be peace in the world,

There must be peace in the nations.

If there is to be peace in the nations,

There must be peace in the cities.

If there is to be peace in the cities,

There must be peace between neighbors.

If there is to be peace between neighbors,

There must be peace in the home.

If there is to be peace in the home,

There must be peace in the heart.

—Lao-tse

Knowing takes you to the threshold,
but not through the door.

—Rumi

"Every work of art stems from a wound in the soul of an artist."
—Ted Hughes

One evening I stayed awake with a problem and painted far into night. I struggled with the image on the canvas. Not knowing where to go, I continued, when suddenly a breast appeared behind the wound with the faint feeling of a heart inside. I really did not know what it meant at the time. But later I learned about the wounded healer.

The story of the wounded healer holds a special place for me. Over time, the spirit can secretly heal our deepest wounds as we grow into adulthood—a kind of soul retrieval. Our earliest wound, once perceived as victimhood, much later changes its form and reveals its true significance.

We live and enjoy our lives. When finally things fall apart, partially or totally, we are pushed into disillusionment. Until today's present disintegrates, we will never uncover what truly will sustain us through thick and thin.

True suffering is the cost of finding the heart at the depth of the wound. The necessary soul suffering that comes from the death of the small-letter self and its birth into the whole Self. When we fight the legitimate fear of being human, our whole Self goes into hiding. But when the depth of the heart is born, we find the sacred wound. Now transformed, the sacred wound becomes a vital ointment for the world, a gift that the original wound has fostered.

Though innocent, not yet wounded, a first-born child is newly formed. The child of a second naiveté, however, has learned the sense of mystery at the cost of her innocence.

The ordinary life journey for each of us becomes a Godly journey. We see the divine in all things, even sin and suffering, and wish to bring our ointment to the growth of the whole world.

Although the universe is whole, at the heart of each individual being in the universe may be a wound. The wound sometimes prevents each of us from knowing that we are whole, are connected, with nobody lost. But mindfulness and meditation can take us beyond it.

PLATE 5: THE WOUND

In the inner stillness where meditation leads,
the Spirit secretly anoints the soul
and heals our deepest wounds.
> —*St. John of the Cross, Mystic*

71

Shifting back into our natural state of joy and peacefulness requires that we become willing to stop the content of thought several times a day and enter into some sort of awareness experience or Stillness Break. By taking a break from the world of analyzing, where ideas can distract and alarm us, we can in short make positive change.

Losing our ability to experience joy may be because of circumstance, but, more frequently, it is blocked by sabotage from the thinking brain and is a deficit in our experience of being in the here and now.

The feeling of peace happens only in the present moment. It is not a state of being we can package and carry home from the past or save for the future. In order to experience peacefulness, we must be willing to be periodically present to our senses within the still moment.

We are all familiar with the coffee break, a time-out for refreshment, one that fuels our metabolism and, if we are fortunate, our psyches as well. Entering a similar, yet very different, time-limited process with the steps described, which I have called the Stillness Break, means a return to the sacred background that underlies all creation, the present moment.

The NOW—beyond the clouds of the temporal—is both the ground and sky of being and the home of consciousness itself.

Entering each Stillness Break provides an opportunity to accept ourselves and our experience "as is" and be grateful. These non-judgmental, periodic visits to the NOW build our connection to the part of our brain that many scientists claim to be the vehicle for experiencing God. In some experiments, researchers have even isolated right-brain activity exhibited in experienced meditators when reporting periods of sacred oneness.

The Stillness Break is a valuable asset to everything we do. It provides a way of balancing our brain activity and connecting us with the nowness of our immediate environment—both external and internal—lasting even after the moments of direct sensory focus are gone.

✦

PLATE 6: AWAKENING

"It's the frames which make some things
important and some things forgotten.
It's all only frames from which content
Rises."
        —Eve Babitz

This periodic moment of stillness, a form of mindfulness, frames and sets aside a picture of our surroundings and separates it from the rest of the background. In the now, we can see, hear, smell, taste, and touch what is here with gratitude. It allows us to appreciate what is caught inside our frame at this time, in this place, and honor it.

"Mindfulness changes the brain," says Dr. Daniel Siegel, psychiatrist and brain researcher. This statement might make us wonder why paying attention in the present moment would change our brain. How we pay attention promotes neural plasticity and creates a change in our neural connections in response to our mindfulness experience, or the Stillness Break. By coming home to the moment, we become more balanced and flexible, and we build up stronger connections to our intuition.

Our moments of still sensory awareness build the physiology of the brain, just as the gym builds our muscles, opening our connection to spirit and divine consciousness.

Enlightenment is not a process of learning. It is a process of un-learning, simply a gift. It is moving to the threshold, out of judging, thinking, and labeling, and entering into the door of knowing through letting go, direct perceiving, and childlike experiencing. As we have discovered, the Stillness Break or traditional mindfulness is a momentary practice that can be used throughout the day; the meditation cushion is not the only "seat" of consciousness.

You do not need to always conceptualize,
interpret,
or label everything
that comes
through your awareness.
                    —Eckhart Tolle

When we can take a break from analyzing and become awakened in the present, the world is unlabeled and fresh. If we need labels they are there for us, but they do not block the experience of being. When thinking, we are labeling, judging, and interpreting rather than perceiving, feeling, and responding, and we are not present.

In the moment, we do not need to judge things to see what is dangerous or bad, our attentive consciousness will let us know what to go near, what to experience from afar, or when to turn away. This happens because we are experiencing a second naiveté, not a first. By this time, we are not uninformed, we have what we need inside us, or we know where to google it. We don't have to judge or interpret life at every moment, we get to respond to it through our consciousness, senses, intuition, and feelings. And we get to live it!

Being present gives us the freedom to be here now, to let others be here as they are, and the world as well—if only in the silent moment. Seeing the weeds as green leaf-forms with pretty tassels for a moment, in the field of no-thought, will not stop us from pulling them up later when weeding the yard.

It is possible to be conscious, to live life through our sense experiences with gratitude, but without identifying with every thought that pops into our head. To experience the holy moment, we must ascend and rise above thought, and we need to! Because being overwhelmed by a word bath of rutted thinking makes us unconscious rather than conscious, blocked rather than alive.

Being in a second naiveté and experiencing as a little child gives us an unblocked present view of the world. We rise above thinking rather than sink below it. This is based not on ignorance but on openness.

To transform

height, width and depth

into two dimensions

is for me an experience full of magic

in which I glimpse

for a moment

that fourth dimension

which my whole being is seeking.

     —Max Beckman

Once upon a time, in the realm where babies come from, there was a little angel, or a fairy, or maybe just a muse. It happened such a long time ago that no one remembers now, but no matter. The point is, she had a very important job. Her job was to hold up a special mirror so that, just before birth, babies could see that they were made in the image of God—a vision that would be a reminder to him or her, when perhaps they had forgotten, of who they were and where they had come from.

Now one day, the little mirror bearer tripped on a pebble just as she was holding the mirror up to the edge of the next divine bassinet, and the mirror flew right out of her hands, fell crashing to the earth, and shattered into as many pieces as there were souls or ever would be. With that, the little mirror bearer began to cry, and her tears fell like a trillion raindrops from the sky—watering the shards and making them smooth so that they slipped in and lodged painlessly inside every human heart where they remain until today.

When we pause, stop talking and thinking, and open the eyes of the heart, we can see who we are, where we came from, and whose image we were made in reflected in each person we meet—yes, even the ones covered with soot, and yes, even if we are a bit sooty ourselves.

And with each meeting we will realize and reaffirm that we are all connected in the sacred light of being by the God within.

Enchantment is born in all of us—

yes, both in you and me,

whether we are artists with paint

or artists with life.

It is to be found in the dialogue between our left and right brain hemispheres and our inner and outer worlds.

Sacred altars rise up for us whenever these four meet. Practicing awareness and our "wholiness" moments will help these four elements come into balance for each of us.

Experiencing art in general is a pathway into the right brain's richness, a balancer for healing the western world's "doing" obsession, a welcoming invitation into a state of "being." Because I am a visual artist, I use the visual arts as the pathway to re-enchantment, peace, and the retrieval of the lost parts of our souls.

Both religious ritual and art derive from the longing to return to and preserve the holy moments of our lives, our experiences of enchantment. These moments happen spontaneously; they surprise us, and we want to hold on to them and make them last, but they slip through our fingers and disappear. Art and ritual are ways to recapture these holy moments. In other words, they are a form of re-enchantment—an attempt to recognize and reach the sacred reality behind the natural world, a reality that we usually judge, label, and dissect.

All of us, at some level, seek to experience the holy moment, electric and alive, to mark it and save it so it can be remembered and revisited again and again.

Art gives us a sense experience—as does nature, our personal environment, our bodies—as well enhancing our lives and blessing our existence in a rich array. Entering its boundaries can serve as a Stillness Break and can carry us out of the trap of monkey mind, the gerbil wheel cycling of our left brains, and return us to balance and wholeness.

Imaginative art—where the inner world of the artist informs but does not duplicate the shape of the world depicted—is one particular method for this escape and the marking of a holy experience. It began far back in prehistory or pre-her-story. During that time, art and religion were closely bound together; mystery and spirit roamed the natural world together.

When imaginative art began, human beings tried to capture the inner spirit of their world by painting on the walls of caves and molding the ground or carving stones into tiny palm-sized goddesses.

Many of the works within these pages continue the ancient tradition of art of this kind. In them, I do not seek to replicate the unattainable perfection of the natural world. The works—by reinterpreting the world rather than imitating it—attempt to surround, catch, and hold the spirit in form, space, and ordinary time.

The great cathedrals, temples, pyramids, and megaliths (such as Stonehenge), all seek to mark, celebrate, and contain the eternal within human history.

PLATE 7: TIME INTERSECTED

In this painting, chronological time—the linear time of history—exists along the horizon, the line of nature and the human journey. The Kairos—nonlinear and timeless—stretches upward and downward beyond ordinary time and space, ascending and descending within the vertical axis of transcendence. Although there are many examples where the holy enters and pierces the ordinary, for me the design of the cross illustrates most clearly the power and meaning of this sacred conjunction.

In my own work, I hope to invite a co-creation, to evoke a dialogue between the perceiver and the perceived—much like in the magic of the theater. Together we step into a liminal space, where one state shifts to another—like steam or twilight or a deck of cards in mid-shuffle. Here we can symbolically defy the gravity, time, and causality of the ordinary world. This co-creative stance, when it connects, can awaken both you and me to the mystical land hidden and waiting beyond the physical landscape, or hidden within the human heart.

The great Abstract Expressionist painter, Mark Rothko, exemplifies this connection in his continuation of this ancient tradition. He articulated a philosophy in which he sought to create a profound connection between himself, his canvas, and the viewer. What's more, he stated that his works not only expressed his own human emotion, but also stimulated a psychological and emotional experience in those of us who witnessed them. Many have reported, including myself, that they have become almost energetically connected in a participatory experience in front of one of his works. Perhaps we become plugged in to something beyond ourselves—what some call the realm of the Spirit?

Although Rothko does not call the relationship between the artist and the viewer a form of co-creation as I do, he describes the experience in his writings as such—saying that people who stand before his works often feel the same feelings he felt while he was painting them. As he once told *LIFE* magazine, "Painting is not about an experience, it is an experience."

Expressionism is a term used, not only for artistic movements, but for expressing the color, light, mood, and feelings of the inner eye. This is sometimes referred to as the third eye or intuition. What the artist experiences on the inside of him or herself is recorded on the outside in visual form—much as in Impressionism the artist records on canvas the light and color and form that is impressed on or seen by the outer eye.

Mystical Expressionism:

A mystic is sometimes defined as a person who finds, by contemplation and self-surrender, a sense of unity with the absolute or the one, and who experiences the truths found beyond the senses and the logical intellect.

When I call myself a mystical expressionist, it implies that my work reflects and expresses unity, a connection of things as one—attempting to access intuitive fields beyond those reached by the intellect or the physical senses alone.

Here we can become aware of the still moment, where we are aware and still and the world moves around us. And, here, for a tiny moment we may experience the wonderful enchantment of being from a position of wholiness.

Wholiness is the fleeting experience of feeling at one—of feeling whole and connected to the unity of all things, to ourselves, to others, to the world, the universe and God as we perceive God.

◆

I believe that the universe is one being,
all its parts are different expressions of the
same energy, and they are all in
communication with each other,
therefore parts of one organic whole.
(This is physics, and believe, as well as
religion.)

—Robinson Jeffers

*If I have to choose one word to describe the
feeling…I would have to say joy…I experience a
feeling of awe when I consider that I am
simultaneously capable of being at one with the
universe, while having an individual identity
whereby I move into the world and manifest
positive change.*

—*Jill Bolt Taylor*

Carl Jung referred to the relationship formed in the bond between persons—the therapist and patient (the artist and the viewer)—as the third soul. Some of you may have experienced that connection in other close relationships. I believe that is what Rothko described here, and what I am naming co-creation, where the viewer/receiver becomes a participant in the creative process.

For me, mystical expressionism lies within the body of art that Jung calls *imaginative* in his iconic book, *Man and His Symbols.* Although this type of art began in prehistory and has continued throughout recorded history (sometimes only in primitive or folk cultures), it certainly lives on today. Here the living spirit resides within the creative process and becomes dormant when the process is finished, only to be kindled alive again within an engagement with the viewer. This is the process of co-creation, when the spirit is revived through a third soul reconnection to the other. The spirit lives and is both fed and held in the relationship between the creator and the perceiver within the arts and beyond.

✦

They say of nature that it conceals with a grand nonchalance,
and they say of vision that it is a deliberate gift,
the revelation of a dancer who for my eyes only flings away her
seven veils.
For nature does reveal as well as conceal. Now-you-see-it,
now-you-don't.
　　　　　　　—Annie Dillard

"Now-you-see-it, now-you-don't" has to do with awareness. One moment you see it, another it's gone. In the flash of an eye!

The Bushmen of the African Kalahari Desert kindle the flame of the spirit in ritual today. They do this by superimposing the imagined events of mythic time, as well as those hewed from human memory, onto their landscape as they tell their stories. Here the landscape becomes animated and is engaged as a living thing. In mystical expression the landscape does the same thing.

A similar animation occurs as Rebecca Wells describes her backyard as filled with little altars. Here we, the receiver of her words, become enlivened with a third soul mystery—found in the oasis of the still moment.

Seven: EXPLORING

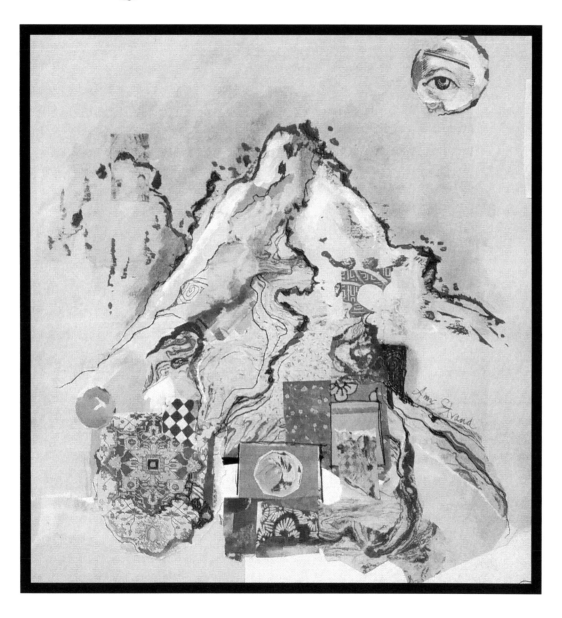

We shall not cease from exploration, and the end of all our exploring will be
to arrive where we started
and know the place for first time.
                    —T.S. Eliot

If there is one thing, I learned…
    it's that imaginal real is entered only through the heart…and so
    by whatever route an exploration leads us, it will stay close to the
    heart. Fortunately, that is not really so difficult…for the heart is
    its native ground.
                    —Cynthia Bourgeault

When the tools of intellectual abstraction have been put into their place, it is native to the child-self, and not so difficult to find. Its tongue is feeling, sensing, and of a deeper order of aliveness that springs from the capital-S Self and its relationship to the universe.

Experiencing art can be as much a creative process as creating it. Exploring art through the senses can be, like exploring nature, another form of the Stillness Break—a break from the normal and our ordinary lives where we incarnate rather than evaluate and enter the breath of stillness through the heart.

When an artist or a piece of art connects us to our hearts, we know! My husband says he feels dizzy in a pleasant way after being immersed in a show by de Chirico or Joseph Cornell.

Taking a time-out during our day to meditatively experience a piece of art through the senses taps into and builds the functioning of the right brain and our connection to spirit. It acts as a break into balance, quiets the word bath of the left brain, and helps create a state of relaxed awakefulness.

Our focus is visual art here, so by letting our eyes enter and journey into a work of art, as if on foot, following the shapes, color, movement, line, and feeling the mood without judgement or labeling, we can shift our internal balance and change the direction of our day.

When we take a time-out and art is around, our regular life experience can be entered by the Kairos, sacred time. Arts of all kinds, when we spend time in experiential focus, stimulate our right brain, and activate the area where the portal to the spirit has its home. Quieting our left brain and experiencing art more directly can begin a journey into the depth of the present moment. Experiencing art through the senses is a form of co-creation. To experience art is to risk delight!

Slip into your senses by viewing a work of art—one in your present surroundings, or one you have come to visit in a museum or a favorite spot of yours—as simply color, movement, shape, line, and texture, as though you were actually walking through it with your eyes.

The mood or atmosphere of the painting may come up as you enter. No judgement. Simply note your feelings and accept them. Go into the colors as you would a grassy meadow or wordless piece of music. Let your eyes flow with the hues, roam the shapes, and enter the crevices. Let your eyes bump over the textures, slide smoothly, or even float into the background atmosphere. Play within its boundaries for a few minutes, riding its lines or brushstrokes and resting in places that bring you pleasure. If words come, enjoy them and let them kindly float out of the picture. No judgement, merely relaxed awakefulness. Surrender to the moment. Later you can think about the artist, the work's period in history, its value. Right now, you are a visitor that does not label or evaluate.

Journeying into the experience of art can become a Stillness Break. Exploring art visually can bring a temporary focus that allows us to experience a level of peace or perhaps delight itself. By taking a moment to experience images, we may be led into the restful holding cradle of the right brain, which in turn brings us into balance.

Entering with sense awareness helps to build the capacity for ongoing presence in our daily lives. A pause of this kind invites us to move into our right hemispheres. Each stop is for a tiny taste of stillness, as we journey into peace, consciousness, and the treasury of our authentic Self.

All true artists,
whether they know it or not,
create from the place of no-mind,
from inner stillness.
　　　　　　　　　　—Eckhart Tolle

The creative process for Jung's "imaginative artist," one who attempts to catch the spirit in matter, is often surprising.

"I don't consider using a quilt unless it is 'lost,' orphaned by its family and extensively flawed, or just a fragment. I think this may come from my fear of being lost myself!"

Although I have been a painter for most of my life, recently I added antique fabrics to my creative storehouse. I find that by rebuilding perishing quilts, mostly Victorian with fancy stitching, with art materials

I have collected over a lifetime, I am honoring the history of feminine art—art for the home and comfort for the soul. My fervent quilt saving is an homage to my aunt, grandmother, and great-grandmother, and all the previous generations of women who were marginalized and unsung as the artists they were. The broken or silent faces embedded within my surfaces invite the viewer to hear the silence and notice the feminine in all people and all things.

Much like a quilter myself—although I am definitely not one—I collect, curate, and attempt to bind together many layers of meaning with my work.

When sorting through a basket of these antique quilt fabrics, they began to speak to me of a favorite childhood memory—playing in the moss-filled chambers of the deep woods, where enchantment filled every crevice, and tiny flowers surprised me one at a time, like fairies.

The fancy stitching on those antique fragments and the brocades reminded me of the sprigs and blossoms of the deep forest, the velvets of the moss, all timeless treasures to refresh and re-enchant the present.

And so a new collaged quilt painting was conceived and born right out of that basket and christened *Deep Forest Glen*. It was given to my son, a scientist, who loved the idea and the quote that went with it!

This…forest, has given me an intimate feeling of the antiquity of the earth. Standing here…I feel a part of a larger…identity; I feel a profound sense of being at home, a sort of companionship with the earth.

—*Oliver Sacks*

Here, scientist and healer Oliver Sacks describes an incarnational experience, being in the here and now. He describes being aware in his body, taking a Stillness Break in nature, just as we can take a Stillness Break by journeying into art.

When an artist works on a piece of art, their eyes may make a journey similar to the stillness meditation I suggested earlier for entering a work of art with your eyes. Taking it all in, the artist may then decide intuitively what will be the next step.

When I began inserting a feminine face into the shattered space of this twentieth-century quilt—with the eyes and mouth separated—I did not realize I was unconsciously echoing the silence that has followed the experiences of women throughout the ages.

The feminine has been silenced throughout "his"tory. Mother Earth and nature, the feminine face of God, and the feminine—in both males and females—has been silenced! This I knew, but I was not aware that theme would appear in this manner.

By honoring these feminine qualities and reclaiming the normal use of our right brain, we can call balance back into the world for all of us—man, woman, child, and earth—and with it, the chance for us to survive as a planet.

✦

PLATE 8: LOOKING BEYOND

I actually felt like everything would
be just fine. Not perfect, but just fine…
And sometimes I believe . . . that the mother who holds me
  isn't Mama.
She's somebody bigger, somebody much older, somebody so tender
  that just looking into her eyes is like a sweet, much needed nap.
She speaks to me daily, this mother, with private signs.
And all I have to do is keep walking, with my ears tuned and my
  eyes wide open.
                              —Rebecca Wells

We must risk delight…
We must have the stubbornness
to accept our gladness
in the ruthless furnace of this world.
                    —*Jack Gilbert*

One day I began to work energetically on a large abstract painting, having in mind the theme of celebration. It was a diptych with two smaller rectangular canvases hung tightly together to form a tall rectangle. I struggled hopelessly to make it into a more profound theme of joy, but the canvases fought back and would not cooperate!

Joy for me contains a darker element than happiness and is longer lasting. Suddenly these words came to me, "Double happiness is a decision."

I separated the canvases, and *Double Happiness* was born, pure and radiant and minus the darkness.

PLATE 9: DOUBLE HAPPINESS

The sole purpose of human existence
is to kindle
a light of meaning
in the darkness…

      —Carl Jung

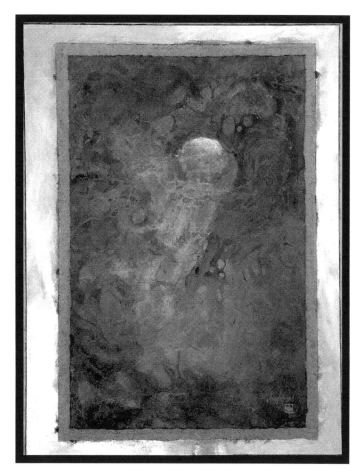

PLATE 10: VIEW FROM THE CAVE

Although this painting began with Plato's Allegory of the Cave as its inspiration, it soon morphed into a journey toward the light. The darkness was overcome by the opening— the mouth of the cave or the proverbial "light at the end of the tunnel." It reminded me of the spark that dwells within and hovers without, as a guide and beacon for each of us—though sometimes, we forget.

Hope is the thing with feathers
That perches in the soul,
And sings the tune without the words
And never stops at all . . .
—Emily Dickinson

PLATE 11: THE COLORS OF HOPE

Years ago, the mystery of this poem captured my imagination and would not depart. The Colors of Hope came about when I was inspired to fray sheer art paper—of coarse plant material, embossed with gold—into feather shapes. The "medium became the message" and the tune became form.

115

Nobody says to a sunflower, "You are dying."
She simply turns her face to the earth
and spills her seeds.
All is ripening on the curve.
(A remembered quotation:)
—Meridel Le Sueur

PLATE 12: THE SUNFLOWER

A friend gave me this orphaned pre-1930s quilt block, mellowed and varied in color and pattern. I found the vintage embroidered sunflower square. Now they are friends in a painting that commemorates the eternal cycle of life spilling life. I have loved this quotation for decades. I wanted to visually honor its richness, its wisdom, and its everlasting love story—an inspiration to the world telling of rebirth and life seeding life, age after age.

117

There are many events
in the womb of time,
which will be delivered.
— *Shakespeare*

Connecting the physical landscape is one of our deepest needs for belonging. It is how we understand our landscape from an outside perspective as well as the one living inside us. The land is not a space one looks at with the eyes alone. It is, above all, the Spirit that interprets what we have seen, heard, felt, and experienced. We therefore attach spiritual meaning and memories to the landscape we have internalized.

"Any landscape is a condition of the Spirit."
—Henri Frederic Amiel

Art as a form of symbolic mapping invites us to explore what might be called the invisible landscape. "Mapping the invisible" is my metaphor for the soul journey that we each make through time and space. Both the internal and external landscapes of our journey are animated or filled with anima, the ancient word for soul. This chapter explores the movement of both the human and artistic journey—together, spilling from the womb of time.

As we pay attention to our mapping, we first come to the spiritual mountain that joins heaven and earth. It is what we expected—and now it stands soaring above us. Within its shadow, we begin to notice strange details. As we travel, we find that the evolving pattern—rather than simply vertical—seems akin to the curving puzzle of the labyrinth.

Here we discover not the obvious linear ascension and permanent arrival of the mountain top experience that we had supposed, but that we are sternly turned, or have turned ourselves, in another direction. The linear pathway seems to give way to the cyclical, for the mountain top, we find, has its secret underground stream and its wandering descent. And, even the ascent can often proceed in small circles, pocketsful again and again—the knit and purl of slowly moving through life's journey.

All these twists and uncertainties make me remember the story of a mountain top sitter who thought he had finally arrived and acclimated to the heights. But then, his visa runs out! So sure of his own stable enlightenment while alone at the pinnacle, now, while at the foot, he might be surprised and irritated to find stress-related beads of sweat on his forehead, or feel tension climbing up and down his spine while standing in the bureaucratic lines needed to renew said visa.

The allegory of the spiritual mountain for the physical one that stands between each soul and its goal is an easy and natural one to make…most people stand in sight of the spiritual mountains… and never enter them. Some travel the mountains with experienced guides…[and] arrive at their destination. Still others…attempt to make their own routes. Few of these are successful, but occasionally some…do make it. Once there they become more aware than any of the others that there is no single or fixed number of routes. There are as many routes as there are individual souls.

—*Robert Pirsig*

✦

PLATE 13: THE SPIRITUAL MOUNTAIN

When painting the spiritual mountain on canvas with many colors, the process became a journey in itself—a struggle—as though I were actually climbing steep walls of stone or paths of crumbling earth. Many trials and errors occurred as I sought to embody Pirsig's quotation—one that had been so comforting to me over the years. But, as I worked, the surface began to get more colorful, less arduous, and touched with gold. Some trails came to an end or just disappeared, but others appeared to make their destination without conflict and even with ease. It seems the journey to the mountain top must always end in letting go, and a reliance on a higher source of peace and love, or it can never be obtained—even for the artist.

But now, our task is recording, and we must continue to mapping the journey. Next, we descend from the mountain top and follow the meandering river as it cuts the valley's velvet belly with the sharp edge of time. Its continuous horizontal ribbon marks our map like the migratory flight of a bird or the coil of the Ouroboros.

The ancient Ouroboros, the snake that bites its own tail, symbolizes the return of all things and tells the unified yet dynamic story of the seemingly eternal changes, faithfully repeating themselves before us moment after moment, year after year and age after age.

> *I was enjoying everything: the rain, the path wherever it was taking me, the earth and the roots beginning to stir. I didn't intend to start thinking about God, it just happened.*
> —Mary Oliver

Virtually all spiritual teachers, in all traditions, have insisted that God is coiled inside us, a tightly wound, subtlety bound energy, that lies within. The names of God lie coiled within the physical forms both inside and outside of us. They cannot appear apart from the sensible realm. Art gives us the change to manifest and name them visually. The interaction, the Third Soul, a conversation with the elements of the universe, that is our job.

When mapping the terrain of the invisible landscape in both my life and artistic journey, I have found that the cycle appears to be the pattern—the movement of all things. Beginning, perhaps, with what appears to be a straight or ascending pathway, while hoping to find a permanent mountain-top experience and solution to our longing—only to return again to find bittersweetly that the life, death, and resurrection cycle of nature is the archetype for each human journey.

The gift of the cycle is its return and rebirth.

If we were to go back and look at the stepping stones of our lives—events that created a change for better or worse—we would no doubt find they formed a circular movement. What we thought was good at the time had a downside, and what we thought was bad an upside, when seen from a distance and through the binoculars of time.

But attention to our mapping must continue as we cycle on and we discover the mellow hills of the second naïveté. Even here, life's ups and downs and arounds repeat themselves and cycle as before—but there is a difference.

During the depths, we can remember to turn within to find the glow of the summer that cannot be destroyed. And that these small invincible summer moments can inform the rest of our day—or perhaps, when repeated, even the rest of our lives.

I realized, through it all that in the midst of winter,
I finally learned there was, within me,
an invincible summer
　　　　　— Albert Camus

A fuller statement of Camus' poetic declaration as it describes his responses to these depths—like the seed that pushes green life from out of the dark earth—indicates a greater power than the depth or the darkness.

In the midst of hate, I found there was, within me,
an invincible love.

In the midst of tears, I found there was, within me,
an invincible smile.

In the midst of chaos, I found there was, within me,
an invincible calm.

I realized, through it all that in the midst of winter, I finally learned
there was, within me,
an invincible summer
and that made me happy.

For it says that no matter how hard the world pushes against me,
within me,
there's something stronger.
Something better, pushing right back.
                          —*Albert Camus*

To me, pushing back seems too dualistic to end with, for the cycle spirals on. Although going back is a part of the cycle, retreating and pushing on is the rhythm of the cycle and return and rebirth is its melody.

◆

So, finally what we find on our journey is that
what was *our beginning is our end.*
But, that in our *end is also our beginning—*
in the times of the seasons,
the resurrecting cycles of nature
and the eternal breath of life.

PLATE 14: THE BREATH TREE

Everything Breathes!

The tree breathes our breath
and gives it
back to us.

Feeling the breath
in the moment
as our lungs expand,
our bodies fill with living molecules
that exchange
with the tree
for life.

133

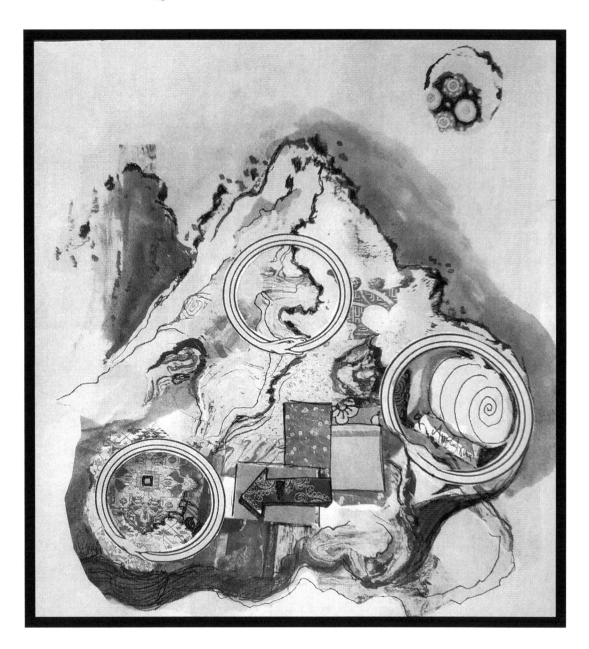

You are accepted.

You are accepted by that which is greater than you,
*   and the name of which you do not know.*

Do not ask for the name now:

Perhaps you will find it later.

Do not try to do anything now.

Perhaps later you will do much.

Do not perform anything. Do not intend anything.

Simply accept the fact that you are accepted!

*   —Paul Tillich*

Life is the art of drawing without an eraser.

*   —John W. Gardener*

O nce I heard a famous guru speak. He stood in front of two thousand people and laughed and said, "It's all very simple, you just bring yourself home, release, and relax." And with that, he began to lift his right arm and hand in a rising circle moving away from himself. At first pause, he reached almost straight out in front of his body and arched his trajectory slightly, as though he was plucking an imaginary fruit hanging off a tree just at the level of his heart, and then he smiled and circling downward brought his hand, now closed as if it had grasped something, back toward his heart. With that motion he said, "Bring yourself home."

Then his hand began to open and rest loosely and limply on his chest over his heart. And with that he said, "Release and relax." Then he repeated the whole thing over and over again in a rhythm that matched normal breathing, moving his arm and hand to the sound and pattern of his words.

Bring yourself home, release, and relax . . . . Bring yourself home, release, and relax . . . . He said it over and over, and we said it with him.

At first I was confused by his actions but now, more than ever, I realize that is what it's all about. Bringing ourselves home in pocketsful of stillness and then bringing ourselves home again, one pocketful at a time, gently and with compassionate acceptance, releasing and relaxing in the process.

We do not get anywhere doing this, we are somewhere.

◆

The entry below is from a 1999 journal of mine—one that, for me, expresses the experience of coming home. I was in my second floor "treehouse" in Oxford Mississippi—after we had returned south again. I had designed a cozy seating nook—that I still miss—high up between two huge trees off the upper deck of our home.

Right now, I sit in silence, a rough bird honks above me, and to my left a call repeats and repeats—trills and scales and chirping come from all directions. It is early, not yet 6 a.m., and the world is awake.

On the road, too far for me to see, I hear the movement of the traffic. I can almost tell what type of creature rolls along the byway by the sound. Again, the honking, mournful now, and constant. It stops and I wonder what has been found.

I look at my feet resting on diagonal boards, weathering the color of barnwood, silver gray. I smell and the smell is of my childhood, a camp smell, moldy sweet and fertile.

I touch the textured bark across from me, covered in sage and purple lichen. This tree is many hued and ancient. It has been waiting for me here a long, long time in silence and will last into the next millennium. It is my companion today.

Beneath me, some of the wildflowers I had planted have come up. It is cool here even when it is hot everywhere else. There is always a breeze. May stretches its arms above me in the form of green leafed branches. I see a blight on the underside of some…

At this moment I am grateful to be in my body in this world. A cardinal sings to me. I do not see him. A truck passes on the road,

141

unseen as well. God is singing to me in this morning, and I have ears to hear and eyes to see.

When we come home to wholiness, the present, and our own heart and breath, we gain the power to teach others to join us and to welcome them into the oneness of reconnection and peace and home. "Home is where the heart is," the old saying goes.

At first it sounds so trite and simple…
       yet the truth is that
    …when we come home
       …we come home in pocketsful
…to our bodies in the present moment
       …to our hearts beating to the
universal breath of being
       …which joins us all.

The most important decision we make

is whether

we believe

we live

in a friendly

or hostile universe.

—*Einstein*

PLATE 15: THE STAINED GLASS UNIVERSE

My inspiration for this piece was a beautiful stained glass rose window. When I began painting, I was horrified to see the image turn into a maudlin sympathy card! The more I tried, the more mired down I became. I had to put the work away for over a year before I could begin again. But when I picked up my brush, my view had expanded, and the window had become the world and then the universe. Time and waiting had somehow taught me that all is connected — that what we see here is reflected beyond us many times over.

All shall be well,
and all shall be well,
and all manner of things
shall be well.

     —*Julian of Norwich*

◯ AFTERWORD

Who looks outside,
dreams.

Who looks inside,
awakes.

—Carl Jung

As we have seen, our capacity to enter the senses—to see, feel, hear, smell, taste, and to enter the being sense of our bodies in the present moment—will increase with our brain's capacity to become more balanced and cycle smoothly left to right and inside to outside and back again. This is the experience of "wholiness."

We are, every single one of us, capable of seeing, sensing, and intuiting so much more than we actually think we can. By taking regular Stillness Breaks, the neural networks in our brain will shift and develop. Suddenly we will stop being in a grey world of black and white but will find ourselves (as we experienced when watching the classic movie *The Wizard of Oz*) vibrating in a technicolor universe.

When I taught drawing, I used to say to my students, "Once you learn to draw you will never see the world in the same way again." But we do not have to take drawing—although I often recommend it in other contexts—because we can literally draw on our receptive brains with repeated practice. We can expand our sense of being, at all levels, because biological science teaches us that when we change one thing, the whole system changes, for good or for ill.

When we choose and act for the good, as poet William Blake tells us, we can "cleanse the doors of perception." The expansion of perception is possible without actually creating art, however, but by fully joining into the process of experiencing the stillness of art, nature, and our immediate surroundings with our open awareness.

We have what we need. We have only to pay attention.

*O*nce upon a time there was a ratty looking beggar sitting on a ratty looking box on the corner of a ratty looking street. He was not paying much attention to the sky, nor to the tiny flowers peeking out from beneath the rubble, or to the pleasant breeze coming his way from over the hill from time to time. In fact, he was not paying very much attention to anything or anyone; he was lost in the regrets of yesterday or in his fears for the future.

Out of nowhere, a strange woman appeared, and the beggar looked up from his low seat, "Lady, can you spare some change?"

The unfamiliar visitor said, "Sorry, I don't any have anything I can give you that would help," but, she just stood silently and didn't walk away.

Again, the beggar asked, and again the visitor refused, but she looked at the beggar very carefully and smiled.

"I am interested in your box," she said, looking at its strange lettering. "Know anything about it?"

Nope," he said.

"Have you ever looked inside it? It looks very old."

"No." he said, "It has been with me forever—almost like I was born with it, but it isn't worth anything except I just like to sit on it."

"Does it ever jingle?" she said.

"I guess a little bit when I move it but it's not a bother. I just don't pay any attention to it."

"Is it heavy?" she said.

"Pretty much, but it's familiar, and it's just the right size."

"If it jingles and it's heavy, I'd have a look inside," she said. "You might have a treasure there."

Of course, when they pried off the end of the box, they discovered it was not empty at all but was filled with many handfuls of gold. Enough to take care of the beggar for the rest of his life.

By now you know that many of us have been like the beggar and like the old song that reminds us "we're looking for love in all the wrong places,"—or in this case, peace, the capacity for wonder, and that feeling of being alive inside. Perhaps, at times, we have not realized that our right brain, the constantly plugged-in instrument of consciousness, spirit, and oneness has been carried around inside us, trying to get our attention, all along. Beggar-like, we may have been lost—all the while clad in a pair of powerful ruby slippers—with no idea that we only had to stand up and to click our heels together to find home.

Really—and I do mean real, as through the senses—experiencing the present moment provides us with the click we need to unlock the door to consciousness.

The stillness pause can break into our unconscious beggar daze and lead us into the golden moment that builds our portal to peace—to the divine realm, hidden and waiting behind the ordinary world.

In the life of the journeyer, the Stillness Break is another way to describe the chance to awaken. It calls us to a "willing suspension of disbelief." Where we are invited to become "true" artists, co-creating our own lives—plugged into and connected to divine consciousness—where right this minute, through the senses, we can find our own sacred altars in a world where "everything is alive and has a secret soul."

Everything…quivers.
Not only the things of poetry,
stars, moon, wood, flowers,
but even a white trouser button
glittering out of a puddle in the street . . .
everything has a secret soul,
which is silent more often than it speaks."
—Wassily Kandinsky

I have little patience with any
philosophy or religion that seeks to
transcend the material realm.
Indeed, the separation of the
spiritual from the material is
instrumental in our heinous
treatment of the material world.
So, when I speak of meeting our
spiritual needs…It is to treat
relationship and…material life itself
as sacred. Because they are.

—Charles Eisenstein, Economist

*I*n parting, I give you these good words—ones that have been important to me. I echo the words above that our relationship to the preciousness of ourselves, others, the earth, and the divine consciousness that holds us all—by whatever name we choose to call upon—cannot be separated. I further affirm the truth of the words below:

The first thing I do to experience my inner peace is to remember that I am part of a greater structure, and eternal flow of energy and molecules from which I cannot be separated.

Knowing that I am part of the cosmic flow makes me feel innately safe and I experience my life as heaven on earth. How can I feel vulnerable when I cannot be separated from the greater whole?

My left mind thinks of me as a fragile individual capable of losing my life.

My right mind realizes that the essence of my being has eternal life…
—Jill Bolt Taylor

It is my experience—and I wish it for you as well—that sometimes in the moment, as we come to our senses—hearing, tasting, smelling, touching, and seeing as little children in their second naïveté—that all the ordinary stuff suddenly seems ordinary no longer, but can become "lit up from inside so that their everyday selves have holy sparks in them," and that the whole world, if just for one golden moment can become filled with wonder!

And my further wish is that, by collecting these moments, your capacity for ongoing presence will grow and you will find the peace that passes all understanding. For we do not see things as they are, we only see things from the eyes of who we are and who we are meant to be. While remembering that

Concerning all acts of initiative
(and creation)

> *there is one elementary truth…*
> *the moment one commits oneself,*
> *then Providence moves too.*

All sorts of things then occur to help one
that would never have otherwise occurred.

> —Goethe

…And that Providence, the creative power of the Universe, is there for us to plug into daily, like that of the Tibetan Wind Horse. The Wind Horse, combining the speed of the wind and the strength of the horse, symbolizes the Immortal Soul.

The divine intelligence of the Wind Horse,
so much greater than our little ego,
   can hoist us
      on its powerful back
 and catch the wind.
Freed from being trapped
in endless worry…
with trusting,
we can grasp its flowing mane,
   defy gravity and fate,
    and fly.

May you rest in Wholiness,

In the cradle of the right brain,

Find hope
   under every fallen leaf,

Rainbows
   within the thunder,

And little sacred altars

Scattered everywhere.

Amen

THE
BEGINNING

My deepest and sincere acknowledgments to:

Author, Rebecca Wells, for lending me the image of the living landscape.

Harvard Brain Scientist, Dr. Jill Bolt Taylor, for explicating the right brain's comforter and for recovering from her stroke to tell us about it.

Artist and Critic, Elaine de Kooning, for her generous and artful manner of teaching.

Theology Professor, Rev. Dr. Nelson S.T. Thayer, for teaching me to meditate and so much more.

Author and Speaker, Eckart Tolle, on how to be momentarily present, still, and aware with all the five senses open.

Educator and husband, Dr. Allan Strand, who believed in me all the way.

Artist, Pat Potter, who read an early copy and gave me wonderful feedback.

Psychologist and Author, Jamie Ungerleider, who read an early copy and gave me the will to go on.

Artist, Promotor, and daughter, Anne Catharine Reeves, who helped me convey my message.

Author, David Tipmore, who read the final copy and gave me support along the pathway.

Computer Consultant, Robert Armstrong, for helping me with Wi-Fi connections.

Editor, Nature Humphries, for treating my words with care, skill, and creativity.

Publisher, Neil White, who believed in and shepherded this book at every stage and brought it through in the time of Covid.

All the wonderful individuals whose quotes have been used to form my artful journey to enchantment.